WONDER & GLORY

60-DAYS OF THRONE ROOM DEVOTIONAL PRAYERS

APOSTLE TONYA

Wonder & Glory: 60-Days of Throne Room Devotional Prayers

Copyright © 2023 Apostle Tonya

All rights reserved. This book is protected by the copyright law of the United States of America and may not be reproduced in any form without written permission.

Scripture quotations are taken from the King James Version and NASB.

The author has purposed to reverenced the Godhead with the use of capitalizing reference of them.

Cover designed by Esther Crown Ministries

For permission requests and reprint, contact: info@esthercrownministries.org

Printed in the United States of America

1 2 3 4 5 6 7 8 9 10

OTHER PRAYER BOOKS BY APOSTLE TONYA

40-Days of Throne Room Prayers
Beneath His Wings: 50-Days of Throne Room Prayers

For Beautiful, Jesus

Dearest Brethren,

Surely, I shall be forever grateful to our most Holy God for the prayers He birthed through me wherefore are included in this third installment of Throne Room Prayers.

As I present this offering unto our Beloved Christ Jesus in a season wherefore I hath endured most great sufferings for His sake; I conclude it most grateful for His strength to pray.

I am most honored for Christ entrusting me to serve each of you. It giveth me joy to impart with the prayers herein my love for Christ, the gospel of God, and also my soul.

Because of the Cross,
Tonya

His work is honourable and glorious:
and His righteousness endureth for ever.
The Book of Psalms 111:3

Day One

Remembering not the former things

Remember ye not the former things, neither consider the things of old. Isaiah 43:18

Eternal Father, I give You thanks and praise for this new day of mercies.

Today I call upon You to grant me grace to remember not the former things, neither consider the things of old. And Father, may You in Your perfection also give me the grace to embrace a new beginning that You have ordained for me.

I bless You for You have made everything beautiful in its time and as I submit to You; You will make my paths straight. In the Name of Christ Jesus, Amen.

Day Two

Signs & Wonders

And it was so: for he rose up early on the morrow, and thrust the fleece together, and wringed the dew out of the fleece, a bowl full of water. Judges 6:38

Kind Father, I give You thanks for the working of Your mighty power, which You wrought in Your Son, Christ Jesus, when You raised Him from the dead, and set Him at Your own Right Hand in the Heavenly Places, far above all principality, and power, and might, and dominion, and every name that is named, not only in this world, but also in that which is to come.

I give You thanks that You have put all things under Jesus' Feet, and gave Him to be the Head over all things to the Church which is His Body, the fulness of Him that filleth all in all.

God, of more than enough, the Bible declares in Isaiah 43:26 this, "Put me in remembrance: let us plead together: declare thou, that thou mayest be justified." Therefore, I want to also put You in remembrance of Your Word in the Book of Judges 6:37-38, which reads: "Behold, I will put a fleece of wool in the floor; and if the dew be on the fleece only, and it be dry upon all the earth beside, then shall I know that thou wilt save Israel by mine hand, as thou hast said. And it was so: for he rose up early on the morrow, and thrust the fleece together, and wringed the dew out of the fleece, a bowl full of water."

Today, God I ask that You release similar instructions and manifestations unto me as recorded in Judges 6:37-38? Would You manifest Your signs for the destiny you have willed for me and my church to fulfill in the earth?

Thank You, Adonai, for giving me the faith that You will answer me. In the Name of Jesus Christ, Amen.

Day Three

Owe no man anything but to love

Owe no man any thing, but to love one another: for he that loveth another hath fulfilled the law. Romans 13:8

Father God, that Hears prayer I give You thanks and praise for Your mighty power, and Your only Begotten Son, Christ Jesus. I give You praise for the Holy Spirit and for His faithfulness to give strength and power unto me and Your people.

Father, in Romans 13:8, the Apostle Paul admonishes that we, "Owe no man any thing, but to love one another: for he that loveth another hath fulfilled the law."

Therefore, I ask that You remember the former things that I have journeyed in life. May You in Your mercy remember the trauma, loss, injustices, and sufferings that I have endured, Father?

Wonder & Glory

Would You in Your mercy visit and heal me from those wilderness seasons? And I ask that as You heal me You would grant me a heart according to Romans 13:8, to owe no man any thing, but to love them.

I praise You for receiving and answering my prayer, Sovereign God. And I seal this prayer with the Blood of the Lord Jesus, Amen.

Day Four

Be my Shield, Father

For the LORD God is a sun and shield: the LORD will give grace and glory: no good thing will He withhold from them that walk uprightly. Psalm 84:11

Father, I arise to give You thanks for this new day that You in Your faithfulness have given to me. I give You thanks for Your only Begotten Son, Christ Jesus and the Spirit of God.

In Psalm, Chapter 84 verse 11, there is a promise which remind me of Your goodness. And it reads: "For the LORD God is a sun and shield: the LORD will give grace and glory: no good thing will He withhold from them that walk uprightly.

Elohim, today I thank You for Your promise of grace and glory. I call upon You and put You in remembrance that Your Word is an entrance of light and it give understanding to the simple. Therefore, I ask that You would be my Shield today and give me grace to be focused in reading the Bible. Thank You for answering me. In Jesus' Name, Amen.

Day Five

Healing Wounds

There is no fear in love; but perfect love casteth out fear: because fear hath torment. He that feareth is not made perfect in love.
1 John 4:18

Merciful Father, I arise this morning to give You thanks for Your only Begotten Son, Jesus Christ who You raised from the dead and set at Your own Right Hand in the Heavenly Places, far above all principality, and power, and might, and dominion, and every name that is named, not only in this world, but also in that which is to come.

Let my cry come before You, Father, as I seek You to remember me, and the soul wounds I have endured because of fear, violence, racial unrest and division in America.

In First John 4:18, the *Holy Bible* reminds me that: "There is no fear in love; but perfect love casteth out fear: because fear hath torment. He that feareth is not made perfect in love."

Wonder & Glory

Therefore, in Jesus' Name I cast out the spirit of fear and loose Your perfect peace according to Isaiah 26:3. I ask that You give me more grace to love without partiality as the Lord's Brother, James writes in James, Chapter 2, verses 1 through 13.

Thank You for answering me, Father. In the Name of the Lion of Judah, Christ Jesus. Amen.

Day Six

Remember the Tabernacles

In the last day, that great day of the feast, Jesus stood and cried, saying, If any man thirst, let him come unto me, and drink.
John 7:37

Holy God, I enter into Your presence with thanksgiving and praise. I declare Your Name is Righteous and Ye are righteous in all Your ways.

I give You thanks for Your only Begotten Son, Jesus Christ who You hath highly exalted and given a Name which is above every name and that at the Name of Jesus every knee should bow, of things in heaven, things in earth, things under the earth and that every tongue should confess that Jesus Christ is Lord to the glory of God the Father.

Father, in John 7:37, Jesus cried, saying, "If any man thirst let him come unto me and drink." This morning, I pray

Wonder & Glory

my cry would come before You for I thirst after You, O God.

I want to also remind You of Your promise in John 14:18 that have caused me to hope. It's this verse that have given me the faith to ask that Your Spirit would come and be a comforter within the midst of my family and church.

Kind God, would You remember the tabernacles of the upright today and cause them to flourish for Your glory?

I bless You Holy God. In Jesus Name, I pray, Amen.

Day Seven

Let not the darkness have dominion over me

And the light shineth in darkness; and the darkness comprehended it not. John 1:5

Elohim, I praise You whom have caused me to arise this morning with new mercies. I praise You for Your only Begotten Son, the Son of God, Christ Jesus whom You have highly exalted and given a Name which is above every Name and at His Name every knee should bow of things in Heaven, earth and under the earth. And I praise You, Father, for the Holy Spirit who is faithful to continue the work of Christ Jesus.

I ask You to Hear my prayer as I cry out to You with confidence and believing by faith that You will receive my prayer and answer me according to Mark 11:23 and 24.

Wonder & Glory

Righteous God, I humble myself before You and exercise power and authority that You have given to me according to Luke 10:19. I decree the Blood of Jesus is a hedge of protection about me in prayer according to Job 1:10.

In John 1:5, it reads: "And the light shineth in darkness; and the darkness comprehended it not."

Therefore, in Jesus' Name I bind the kingdom of darkness comprehending the light of Christ which shines upon me. I declare the enemy have no dominion over me. I declare I will remain hidden in Jesus Christ. It's in His Matchless Name, I seal this prayer, Amen.

Day Eight

Thanksgiving for the Holy Spirit

O give thanks unto the Lord, for He is good: for His mercy endureth for ever. Psalm 107:1

Abba Father, I enter into Your gates with thanksgiving, into Your courts with praise and bless Your Name. I praise You for Your mercy, grace and for allowing me to hear Your lovingkindness every morning.

I want to thank You for the verse recorded in John 14:16: "And I will pray the Father, and He shall give you another Comforter, that He may abide with you for ever."

Father, I thank You for Your Son, Jesus Christ' promise in this verse to the Disciples that He would pray for another Comforter who would abide with them forever. And I

Wonder & Glory

praise and honor You for sending the gift of the Holy Spirit who dwell in me.

Holy Spirit, I give You thanks for enabling me to walk in truth and for Your comfort, joy, peace and presence which by Your grace I pray will remain in and upon me.

Thank You for mercy that endureth forever. In the Name of Christ Jesus, Amen.

Day Nine

Prayer for my enemies

And there came also Nicodemus, which at the first came to Jesus by night, and brought a mixture of myrrh and aloes, about an hundred pound weight. John 19:39

Righteous God, who Hears prayer, in the multitude of Your tender mercies I call upon You today. I pray believing You will answer my petition according to Mark 11:24 which reads: "Therefore I say unto you, what things soever ye desire, when ye pray, believe that ye receive them, and ye shall have them."

I put You in remembrance of Your Word according to John 19:39-40. In this passage, Nicodemus was granted the courage to depart from Your enemies and helped to prepare our Lord's Body for His Burial.

Father, I bless You for giving Nicodemus a heart to love our Lord more than the traditions of men. And I cry out to You to remember me and open the eyes of the enemies who seek

Wonder & Glory

to destroy me; fighting against Your will for my life.

I ask You to cause their hearts to turn away from wickedness and give them pure love for me as You were generous to impart into the heart of Nicodemus. I bless You that in the end; Nicodemus loved Jesus more than the Jews. Let this blessing also be for my enemies, O Lord.

Let all the earth fear and stand in awe of You. In the Name above every name, Christ Jesus, I pray. Amen.

Day Ten

May my prayers pass through

I will praise the LORD according to His righteousness: and will sing praise to the Name of the LORD most high. Psalm 7:17

Righteous God, I pray that You would defer not to answer me as I call upon You today. In Your great mercy and compassion I come before thee to ask that You would remove the cloud that Thou might have coverest Thyself so my prayers should not pass through as written in Lamentations 3:44?

I thank You for Hearing this cry, Father, and for Your forgiveness. I reverence, honor and bless Your Holy Name. In Jesus' Name, Amen.

Day Eleven

Strong tears

Though He were a Son, yet learned He obedience by the things which He suffered; Hebrews 5:8

Merciful Healer, I ask You to Hear my cry and answer me as I offer my sacrifices of praise to You.

In the Book of Hebrews 5:7-8, it records that You offered up prayers and supplications with strong tears to Your Father and were heard in that You feared. Today I am encouraged by Your obedience in that time to the Father and ask that You remember the afflictions and sicknesses of my sisters and brothers who the enemy have oppressed.

Jesus, may You with Your glory and power heal them? For I declare You alone are the Lord that can heal. I praise You for the manifestations of healing and restoration for all my friends and neighbors who are in need. Ye are holy and merciful, Lord. Amen.

Day Twelve

Abounding in Thanksgiving

As ye have therefore received Christ Jesus the Lord, so walk ye in Him: Rooted and built up in Him, and stablished in the faith, as ye have been taught, abounding therein with thanksgiving. Colossians 2:6-7

Good Father, we come before You to bless Your glorious and wonderful Name. As my family and me prepare to feast in the *Holy Bible*; I pray that You in Your lovingkindness would give each of us tender hearts for You.

It is our pray that we fear You and always invite the Spirit of God to teach us the truth, open our eyes of understanding and bless us with wisdom.

In this time of our precious fellowship with you, may Your Spirit cause us to abound in thanksgiving, walk in unity, forgiveness, and in Your love.

Thank You, Christ Jesus, for being in the midst. Its in Your Blood that we seal this prayer, Amen.

Day Thirteen

Holy unto Thee

And ye shall be holy unto me: for I the LORD am holy, and have severed you from other people, that ye should be mine. Leviticus 20:26

Jehovah-Mekadesh, I enter into Your gates with thanksgiving and Your Courts with praise. I give You thanks for Your only Begotten Son, Jesus who You have highly exalted, and given Jesus a Name which is above every name. At Jesus' Name every knee should bow, of things in Heaven, things in earth, things under the earth and that every tongue should confess that He is Lord.

Today I arise to call upon You, the Lord who Sanctifies to have respect unto my prayer and hearken unto me.

First, I praise You that You have not called me to walk in the earth for the purpose of impurity, but in sanctification.

Wonder & Glory

And I praise You for the *Holy Bible* records in Leviticus 20:26: "And ye shall be holy unto me: for I the LORD am holy, and have severed you from other people, that ye should be mine."

So, God, I pray that You would sanctify me and that Your righteous eyes would see not anything indecent in me to make You to turn away.

May this prayer of faith please You. In the Name of Jesus, I pray, Amen.

Day Fourteen

The Children's Bread

Continue in prayer, and watch in the same with thanksgiving.
Colossians 4:2

Jehovah Gibbor, I offer You my sacrifice of praise; mighty and righteous, God.

In Acts, Chapter 10 verse 38, it reads: "How God anointed Jesus of Nazareth with the Holy Ghost and with power: who went about doing good, and healing all that were oppressed of the devil; for God was with Him."

Today I cry out to You to remember my sisters and brothers who are held in the bondage of oppression with bears lying in wait for them and also lions in secret places. May You in Your eternal power which is greater than the adversary; deliver and redeem them from this oppression, Jehovah God?

Wonder & Glory

I thank You for hearing this prayer and granting the desires of the hearts of my sisters and brothers-in-the-Lord who are oppressed.

I pray that You would also remember to give them who are weary rest, and joy that You promised in the *Holy Bible* that come with Your answers. In the Name of the Jesus, our Savior, Amen.

Day Fifteen

Toucheth His Garment

And a woman having an issue of blood twelve years, which had spent all her living upon physicians, neither could be healed of any. Luke 8:43

Righteous God, who is Enthroned above the cherubim, I declare that You are God. I plea with You to answer me as I call upon thee today and come boldly unto Your Throne of Grace to obtain Your tender mercy, find grace and Your resurrection power to pray for healing.

In the *Holy Bible*, Christ Jesus attended to the sick and oppressed with compassion and mercy which have encouraged me to pray for myself and others. One passage I want to bring to Your remembrance is in Luke 8:43-44.

In these verses, it records of the faithful testimony of a woman having an issue of blood for twelve years who exhausted her finances seeking to be healed from physicians and could not be healed for the grip of the spirit of infirmity.

Wonder & Glory

I thank You for Your mercy to help this woman of faith and give her the strength to not only journey to Jesus, but to touch the border of the Healer's garment.

This miracle continue to build my faith for the healing and miracles needed for my sisters and brothers-in-the Lord and me. Therefore, I ask You to remember this story of great faith as we battle with our afflictions.

Healer, in Your mercy I pray that You would bless us with healing, and a swift miracle. Thank You for hearing my cry, in Jesus' Name, I pray, Amen.

Day Sixteen

Grant me skill and understanding

And he informed me, and talked with me, and said, O Daniel, I am now come forth to give thee skill and understanding. Daniel 9:22

Merciful God, I enter into Your gates with thanksgiving and Your Courts with praise.

Father, in the Book of Daniel, Chapter 9, the *Holy Bible* records that Daniel confessed his sins and that of Israel in prayer. And while Daniel was in prayer You sent the archangel, Gabriel with a message for him to give Daniel skill and understanding.

I give You thanks for this encouragement in Daniel. Today I ask that You would grant me a visitation from an angel in my sleep to give me skill and understanding on how to serve You in the Body of Christ. In Jesus' Name, Amen.

Day Seventeen

Remember the Word You Promised

And, behold, I am with thee, and will keep thee in all places whither thou goest, and will bring thee again into this land; for I will not leave thee, until I have done that which I have spoken to thee of. Genesis 28:15

Jehovah-Mekadesh, on this morning of wonder I ask that Your Spirit cause my mouth to be filled with spontaneous worship for You. For who is like You, O Lord, among the gods? Who is like You, glorious in holiness, fearful in praises, doing wonders?

In Genesis, Chapter 28, verse 15, it reads: "And, behold, I am with thee, and will keep thee in all places whither thou goest, and will bring thee again into this land; for I will not leave thee, until I have done that which I have spoken to thee of."

Mighty God, who sits on the Throne would You remember to perform the Word You have promised to me? And I will wait upon thee, and in Your Word do I hope. In Jesus' Name, Amen.

Day Eighteen

Prayer for Righteous Leaders

In every thing give thanks: for this is the will of God in Christ Jesus concerning you. 1 Thessalonians 5:18

Holy Jesus, I arise to give You thanks for granting Your blessing upon me today. I am grateful for this new day that in Your faithfulness You have given to me to glorify You.

Early this morning, I come before You to pray for Your shepherds and overseers. I thank You for choosing them to serve You and the Body faithfully with joy and gladness. And today I ask that You remember my pastor and give him strength, wisdom and grace to continue to lead righteously.

May You in Your goodness release faithful pastors in this End Time to watch for the souls as it is recorded in Hebrews 13:17? May You also remember to give strength to Your apostles, prophets, teachers and evangelists today, Lord. In Your Name Jesus, I pray, Amen.

Day Nineteen

Thy Word I will keep in my Soul

Thy testimonies are wonderful: therefore doth my soul keep them. Psalm 119:129

Father, I put You in remembrance that Your Word is an entrance of light and it gives understanding to the simple? And I am certainly blessed with the verse today in the Book of Psalms 119:129 which reads: "Thy testimonies are wonderful: therefore doth my soul keep them."

May I ask that You bless me with Your light and understanding as I study Your Word as it is written in Psalm 119:130?

I declare the Bible shall be kept in my soul according to Psalm 119:129. Thank You for receiving this prayer, Gracious Father. I give You thanks forever. In Jesus' Name, Amen.

Day Twenty

Release a New Sound

*Who shall ascend into the hill of the LORD? or
who shall stand in his holy place?* Psalm 24:3

Holy God of Abraham, Isaac and Jacob who dwell between the cherubims, I serve You with fear, and rejoice with trembling for Ye are holy.

On this day that You have made for Your glory; I arise to bless You for Your Son, Jesus, the Word who became flesh; full of grace and truth. And God, I bless You for the faithfulness of the Holy Spirit.

In Jesus' Name, I declare I will worship You alone, sing of Your eternal love, and proclaim Your mighty power. I ask that You in Your lovingkindness would release Your riches from Heaven upon me and believers.

Wonder & Glory

Holy God, would You consider this petition and release a new sound that You would take pleasure in?

Thank You for receiving and answering my prayer, God. I seal this prayer with the Blood of Jesus, Amen.

Day Twenty-One

I pray for Your unfailing love

Blessed are the undefiled in the way, who walk in the law of the LORD. Psalm 119:1

Holy Jesus, whom righteousness belong I arise to give You praise.

In the *Holy Bible*, I am held in awe of Your holy, righteous and disciplined life of prayer. And it continue to encourage me to arise while it is yet dark; in the cool of day, to seek You. For the Bible declares that those that seek You early shall find You.

Today I ask You to let the blessings of the morning continue to bring me word of Your unfailing love for me. And Lord, would You grant me more grace of Your attributes of lowliness and gentleness? Thank You for answering my prayer, Jesus. Amen.

Day Twenty-Two

Give me Your Joy

These things have I spoken unto you, that My joy might remain in you, and that your joy might be full. John 15:11

Jesus Christ, who is Enthroned in Heaven seated at the Right Hand of Your Father; I give You all the praise, honor and glory.

In Hebrews 12:2, I read in awe that for the joy which was set before You; You braved the greatest suffering at the Cross. On this morning that You have granted to me to live for Your glory; I desire to read to You what Your Word says in John 15:11, the verse says: "These things have I spoken unto you, that my joy might remain in you, and that your joy might be full."

Jesus, thank You for this Scripture which You have given to me to know reading the Gospels imparts joy. I ask the Comforter bless me with the fruit of the Spirit of joy remembering this verse in John and according to Galatians 5:22. In Your Name, Jesus, I pray, Amen.

Day Twenty-Three

Prayer for Governors

I exhort therefore, that, first of all, supplications, prayers, intercessions, and giving of thanks, be made for all men; For kings, and for all that are in authority; that we may lead a quiet and peaceable life in all godliness and honesty. 1 Timothy 2:1-2

Holy God, in You we trust; and together declare all thy works shall praise You, and thy saints shall bless You. We bless You this morning for the Son, Jesus Christ, and the Holy Spirit.

Today we ask You to remember the government in the fifty states in the United States. May You in your mercy grant the governors guidance, and wisdom? May You give them hearts to lead a quiet and peaceable life in all godliness and honesty?

Merciful God, we declare over this nation, Psalm 33:12, "Blessed is the nation whose God is the LORD; and the people whom He hath chosen for His own inheritance". In faith and encouraged of Your mercy, we seal this prayer with the Blood of Jesus, Amen.

Day Twenty-Four

Fill my mouth with Your praises

O LORD, our Lord, how excellent is thy name in all the earth! who hast set thy glory above the heavens. Psalm 8:1

Eternal Father, whom rules and reigns, I bless You for Your splendor, excellency and glory. How awesome is it that You have established the clouds above and swirl them around over the face of the whole earth to do whatever You command.

In awe of Your creation, I arise in this morning of wonder and glory to bless You for inhabiting my praises, and to simply be still. In Jesus' Christ Name, Amen.

Day Twenty-Five

Show me Your Glory

And he said, I beseech thee, shew me thy glory. Exodus 33:18

Dear Jesus, I arise to give You thanks for granting Your blessing upon me on this new day that in Your faithfulness You have given to me to glorify You in the earth.

On this morning of awe and wonder, I pray that I will find grace in Your sight to stand before Your holy presence and behold Your glory. For my heart desires to gaze upon You, Lamb of God.

I bid You to shew me Your glory. Amen.

Day Twenty-Six

Sanctify me in thy truth

Sanctify them through thy truth: thy word is truth. John 17:17

Holy Father, I thank You for this day which you hath given to me to worship You. Today I pray that You in Your lovingkindness would sanctify me in Your truth according to the passage in John 17:17.

I thank You for answering me as I call upon You with confidence that You will take pleasure in sanctifying me in thy truth for Your glory. In the Name of Your Son, Jesus Christ, Amen.

Day Twenty-Seven

Grant me Your peace

Peace I leave with you, my peace I give unto you. John 14:27

Wonderful Jesus, whom righteousness belong, I arise in the womb of the morning to give You all the praise, honor and glory.

In the Book of John 14:27, the Scripture records of Your impartation of peace to the Disciples. It reads: "Peace I leave with you, my peace I give unto you: not as the world giveth, give I unto you. Let not your heart be troubled, neither let it be afraid."

Therefore, I ask You, Lord of Peace in Your lovingkindness to grant me an abundant of peace even according to the Word. Thank You for Your kind answer. In Your Name Christ, I pray, Amen.

Day Twenty-Eight

Grace not to look Backwards

Thou hast turned for me my mourning into dancing. Psalm 30:11

Merciful Father, give Ear to my prayers as I remember my past seasons of distress which I have journeyed to partake in Jesus' sufferings.

I bless You for the strength I received from reading and meditating on Bible verses. In particular, Psalm 30:11, which reads: "Thou hast turned for me my mourning into dancing: thou hast put off my sackcloth, and girded me with gladness."

God, I thank You that just as You delivered David, the psalmist in the *Holy Bible*, You have delivered me. So, on this day I bless You for restoring hope, strength, and encouragement. Thank You for giving me the grace not to look backwards at the past seasons of mourning and loss; but to keep my eyes beholding upon You.

I pray that I remember to give You thanks forever. In Jesus' Name, Amen.

Day Twenty-Nine

Creation Glory

And now, O Father, glorify thou me with thine own self with the glory which I had with thee before the world was. John 17:5

Father of Glory, in John 17:5, Jesus prayed with His Disciples that You would glorify Him with the glory He had with You before the world was.

Today I arise with awe and gratitude of Christ Jesus' prayer. I ask that in generosity You would glorify thyself with the same creation glory before the world was as Jesus prayed.

I give You praise, and honor for hearing my prayer. In the Name of Jesus, I thank You for answering. Amen.

Day Thirty

King of Glory, Visit us

After these things Jesus shewed Himself again to the disciples at the sea of Tiberias; and on this wise shewed He Himself. John 21:1

King of Glory, I give You thanks in this dawn of the morning for a new day that I will begin by Your grace and for Your glory.

Certainly, it's precious to read in the Gospels of Your patience and teachings to Your Disciples and Followers. Encouraged by the profound passage in Hebrews 13:8, I come before thee to humble myself also remembering John 21:1.

Therefore, Jesus, I ask You if would remember my church and bless us with Your holy and cherished presence. Amen.

Day Thirty-One

Be glorified in my good works

Let the words of my mouth, and the meditation of my heart, be acceptable in thy sight, O LORD, my strength, and my redeemer. Psalm 19:14

Jehovah El Roi, I bless Your Holy Name and arise to give You praise, glory and honor.

Today I pray You would give me grace to do that which is good and pleasing in Your Sight and that You would be glorified in my good works.

I am encouraged that as I call upon You; You will answer me and show me great and mighty things, which I know not according to Jeremiah 33:3.

I thank You, Jehovah for Your faithfulness, kindness and mercy. I seal this prayer with the Precious Blood of the Lamb of God. Amen.

Day Thirty-Two

Bless me Reading thy Word

Blessed is he that readeth, and they that hear the words of this prophecy, and keep those things which are written therein: for the time is at hand. Revelation 1:3

Lord God, I call upon You to ask that in Your loving-kindness You would bless me with revelation when I read the *Holy Bible*. Would you consider this petition, God?

And I pray You would grace me with humility to read, and memorize Your Word. Thank You for hearing this prayer. In Jesus' Name, I seal this prayer. Amen.

Day Thirty-Three

Let my worship glorify You

I beseech you therefore, brethren, by the mercies of God, that ye present your bodies a living sacrifice, holy, acceptable unto God, which is your reasonable service. Romans 12:1

Father God, on this day that You have made for Your glory; I arise to bless You for Your Son, Jesus Christ of Nazareth, the Word who became flesh; full of grace and truth and also for the faithfulness of the Comforter.

Today I declare I will sing of Your eternal love, and proclaim Your power in the earth. Knowing that I can do all things through Christ that strengthened me; I ask You in Your lovingkindness to release a pure sound in my heart to worship You.

I declare I shall worship You in spirit and in truth according to John 4:24. In the Name of Jesus Christ. Amen.

Day Thirty-Four

My Vow to Keepeth

If a man vow a vow unto the LORD, or swear an oath to bind his soul with a bond; he shall not break his word; he shall do according to all that proceedeth out of his mouth. Numbers 30:2

Lord Jesus, in the *Holy Bible*, I am oftentimes held in awe of Your righteous and disciplined life of prayer to Your Father.

Today I ask that You give me the strength, and discipline to be faithful in my commitment to You in morning prayer. Remembering that the Bible encourages me to seek thee early in the morning, I pray that You would give me a heart to honor thy word and to keep my vows to You.

May I be faithful in the appointed time of morning prayer to seek You according to Romans 12:12. Amen.

Day Thirty-Five

Heal me, O God

For I will restore health unto thee, and I will heal thee of thy wounds, saith the LORD; because they called thee an Outcast, saying, This is Zion, whom no man seeketh after. Jeremiah 30:17

Father, I desire to bring to Your remembrance a verse in Jeremiah, Chapter 30, verse 17, which records a declaration of Your promise. The verse reads: "For I will restore health unto thee, and I will heal thee of thy wounds, saith the Lord; because they called thee an Outcast, saying, This is Zion, whom no man seeketh after."

Certainly, I praise You for this promise of healing, God. By faith, I rebuke the evil spirit of infirmity that has attacked my body. In Jesus' Name, and according to Luke 9:1, I loose Your resurrection power to heal me as I lay upon my bed of languishing.

Thank You, Father, for Your mercy. In the Name of Your Son, Jesus, Amen.

Day Thirty-Six

Praise for God, the Rock of our Refuge

*But the LORD is my defence; and my God is
the rock of my refuge.* Psalm 94:22

Jehovah Gibbor, as Decreed in Philippians 2:9-10: You hath highly exalted Your Son, Christ Jesus and given Him a Name which is above every Name and at His Name every knee should bow, of things in heaven, earth and under the earth.

In Jesus' Name, I praise You for the power and authority You have bestowed upon me to tread on serpents and scorpions. I thank You for the hedge of protection that surrounds me according to Job 1:10. And I declare according to Ephesians 6:10-18, I am clothe with the full armor of God.

Today I give you praise for my protection in the earth and for being my refuge according to Psalm 94:22. Strengthen in my faith by the Word, I declare I have victory over the enemy's wicked devices, and plots against me.

Thank You, Jehovah for this victory. In the Name of Your Son, Jesus, Amen.

Day Thirty-Seven

Redeeming time Loss

Redeeming the time, because the days are evil.
Ephesians 5:16

Jehovah Tsidkenu, the Lord our righteousness, I exalt You and declare I shall bless Your Holy Name forever. I thank You that You sent Your Son, Jesus Christ of Nazareth to restore my hope, and heal my brokenheart from the wounds incurred from the delay of the manifestations of Your promises.

In Christ Jesus' Name, I command the angels to cometh for my words according to Daniel 10:12, and redeem the time the enemy unlawfully have taken from me which resulted in losses in my life not according to Your will.

Thank You for Your righteous judgment and for answering my cries. In the Name of Your Son, Jesus. Amen.

Day Thirty-Eight

My Hiding Place

Thou art my hiding place; thou shalt preserve me from trouble; thou shalt compass me about with songs of deliverance. Selah.
Psalm 32:7

Kind Father, I give You thanks for a Bible verse which have continued to encourage and remind me of Your faithfulness to preserve me. Can I read it to You, Father? It's in Psalm 32:7 and reads: "Thou art my hiding place; thou shalt preserve me from trouble; thou shalt compass me about with songs of deliverance. Selah."

On this womb of the morning, I want to thank You for this passage which comforts me, and remind me of Your faithfulness toward me. And Father, I bless You for Your angels who come for my words in prayer to protect me from the secret counsel, plots, wicked strategies and conspiracies of the enemy.

Thank You for being my Fortress, Protector, and Hiding Place, Father God. I appreciate Your loving concern for me. In Jesus' Name, Amen.

Day Thirty-Nine

Keep me from idolatry

Thou shalt have no other gods before me.
Exodus 20:3

Holy God, I call upon You today to ask that Your Spirit give me grace to remember to walk boldly as a lion against the worship of man, wealth, possessions, food, and social media according to Exodus 20:3.

Certainly, Father, I tremble as I read the passage in Exodus 34:14, that Thou Name is Jealous, and Thou art a Jealous God. Therefore, I beg You to give me a heart to keep myself from idolatry and to bow and worship You alone.

May I be faithful to keep Your commandment as recorded in Mark 12:30, and love You with all of my heart, soul, mind, and with all of my strength. In Christ Jesus' Name, Amen.

Day Forty

Thank You for the Comforter

And I will pray the Father, and He shall give you another Comforter, that He may abide with you for ever. John 14:16

Dear Father, I arise today with thanks for You, Your only Begotten Son, Jesus, and the Holy Spirit. I thank You for the verse in John 14:16 which I am sure will encourage me throughout the day. The Son of God says in this passage: "And I will pray the Father, and He shall give you another Comforter, that He may abide with you for ever."

I praise You for the promise in this verse from Christ. I give You thanks for Christ' concern and compassion for me. I give You thanks for the sending of the Holy Spirit and His patience even when I may not always be patient or kind to Him.

And I praise You for the Spirit of God's faithfulness to make intercession for me with groanings which cannot be uttered according to Romans 8:26. In Jesus Name, Amen.

Day Forty-One

Answer me, O God

Thy prayers and thine alms are come up for a memorial before God.
Acts 10:4

Heavenly Father, I arise with new mercies to bless You for Your faithfulness, and for the Lordship of Jesus Christ.

In Christ' Name, I come before Your throne to ask that You remember Your Word sent by Your angel to Cornelius, during his time of fasting. In this verse, which is recorded in Acts 10:4, the angel stood before Cornelius and declared to him: "Thy prayers and thine alms are come up for a memorial before God."

How great it is for me to read of Your response to Cornelius prayers and alms, Father. I am encouraged of Your generosity and that You gave Cornelius more than he asked of Thee. Therefore, knowing that you You are nigh to those that call upon You in truth I ask You to answer my prayers supernaturally just as You answered, my brother, Cornelius.

Thank You for receiving my prayer, Father. I am grateful for the Spirit of God and expectant of Your answers to bless my family and me. In the Name of Jesus, Amen.

Day Forty-Two

The Wings of this Morning

If I take the wings of the morning, and dwell in the uttermost parts of the sea; even there shall thy hand lead me, and thy right hand shall hold me. Psalm 139:9-10

Holy God, I rise on this morning of awe and wonder to give You the praise, honor and glory. I give You thanks for leading me to hear Your lovingkindness today. And I give You thanks for the comfort, patience, and kindness of the Holy Spirit.

I am most encouraged with the verses recorded in the Book of Psalms, Chapter 139 verses nine through ten. I give You thanks for this Word for it has given me confidence that as I seek to take the wings of this morning Your Right-Hand will hold me.

Therefore, God, I pray my voice and supplication be efficacious and acceptable in Your Sight. I ask You according to the riches of Your glory to be strengthened with might by Your Spirit in my inner man according to Ephesians 3:16.

Wonder & Glory

Kind God, there's one more request I want to ask of You this morning, may You help me to always have gratitude for the Incarnate Son of God, the Cross and Jesus' triumphant Resurrection? It is in the Name of the Lord Jesus, I pray, Amen.

Day Forty-Three

Let me not frustrate the grace of God

I do not frustrate the grace of God: for if righteousness come by the law, then Christ is dead in vain. Galatians 2:21

Righteous God, how I am in awe of Your holiness, goodness and of Your Son, the Risen Lord whom You have sent.

How blessed is the Scripture in the Book of Galatians 2:21 which reads: "I do not frustrate the grace of God: for if righteousness come by the law, then Christ is dead in vain."

Father, I give You thanks for Your word in Galatians. I ask that You hear my cry and enable me not to frustrate the grace of God.

I pray that I may have grace to remain in the Spirit and my heart be Your dwelling place today. In Jesus' Name, Amen.

Day Forty-Four

May my Light Shine

Let your light so shine before men, that they may see your good works, and glorify Your Father which is in heaven. Matthew 5:16

Righteous God, on this day that You have granted me to serve You, I am thankful for the guidance of the Holy Spirit. I am also thankful for the Scripture in Matthew 5:16, which Jesus Christ command: "Let your light so shine before men, that they may see your good works, and glorify Your Father which is in heaven."

I thank You for the words of Jesus which will encourage me as I meditate on it throughout my day. It is also my prayer that as I seek to be sensitive to the Holy Spirit to witness of Jesus today, my light will shine before men. In Jesus' Name, Amen.

Day Forty-Five

Purify Me

Who gave himself for us, that He might redeem us from all iniquity, and purify unto Himself a peculiar people, zealous of good works.
Titus 2:14

Heavenly Father, I am in awe of You for Ye are a holy, righteous and powerful God. In this early morning, I rise with Jesus' Heart to pray while it is yet dark. And I ask that You would redeem and purify me from my sins, transgressions and iniquity as recorded in Titus 2:14.

May You purify and present me faultless before the presence of Your glory, Father?

Thank You for hearing this prayer according to 1 John 5:14-15. In the Name of Your, Son, Jesus Christ, Amen.

Day Forty-Six

Lord, I welcome You into my home

Now it came to pass, as they went, that He entered into a certain village: and a certain woman named Martha received Him into her house. And she had a sister called Mary, which also sat at Jesus' feet, and heard His word. Luke 10:38

Holy Jesus, I pray that the Spirit of God would enlighten me to know when one thing is needful and when to chose to rest at Your Feet just as my foremother, Mary. And may You give me a heart to keep Your presence in my home as it appears it was with her sister, Martha according to Luke 10:38-42.

By faith, I also desire to ask that You would remember my family and church family and continue to encourage them to pursue You and rest in Your presence. May You keep us clothed in Your humble garments so we will serve others without being troubled about many things. In Your Name Jesus, I pray, Amen.

Day Forty-Seven

Come with healing in Your Wings

But unto you that fear My name shall the Sun of righteousness arise with healing in His wings; and ye shall go forth, and grow up as calves of the stall. Malachi 4:2

Father God, I declare that You are nigh unto all that call upon You, to all that call upon You in truth.

Therefore, in the Lord Jesus' Name, I summon Your power and declare the Sun of Righteousness will be merciful and visit me with healing in His wings to heal my body from the suffering of sickness and disease.

I praise You for Your mercy to remember me and heal my body. In Jesus' Blood, I seal this prayer, Amen.

Day Forty-Eight

I declare I will be fruitful

And God blessed them, and God said unto them, Be fruitful, and multiply, and replenish the earth, and subdue it: and have dominion over the fish of the sea, and over the fowl of the air, and over every living thing that moveth upon the earth. Genesis 1:28

Generous God, I declare this is the day which You hath made; and I will rejoice and be glad in it.

I declare this day You have orchestrated in Heaven for me to be fruitful according to Genesis 1:28. I declare I will honor Your will for me and walk worthy of You, fully pleasing You, and being fruitful in every good work.

Thank You for hearing my prayers, God. In the Name of Your Son, Jesus, I seal this prayer. Amen.

Day Forty-Nine

Wisdom from Above

If any of you lack wisdom, let him ask of God, that giveth to all men liberally, and upbraideth not; and it shall be given him.
James 1:5

Father, I praise You for causing me to hear Your lovingkindness this morning. By faith, I ask You to remember the Book of James 1:5 and that You would give me wisdom from heaven which is pure, peaceable, gentle, easy to be intreated, and full of Your mercy according to James 3:17.

As You remember me with Your answer, I pray that You would grace me to be a good steward of the wisdom that You give to me. And I ask that You would give me a heart to honor Your gifts and to never touch Your glory. In the Name of Your Son, Jesus Christ. Amen.

Day Fifty

A heart that loves purity

He that loveth pureness of heart, for the grace of his lips the king shall be his friend. Proverbs 22:11

Father God, I extol You and thank You for hearing my prayer. In Proverbs 22:11, it reads: "He that loveth pureness of heart, for the grace of his lips the king shall be his friend."

In this blessed morning, I pray that You would give me a heart that loves purity and that will forever please You.

I thank You for answering me. In the Name of the Lord Jesus Christ, Amen.

Day Fifty-One

Holy Thoughts

Finally, brethren, whatsoever things are true, whatsoever things are honest, whatsoever things are just, whatsoever things are pure, whatsoever things are lovely, whatsoever things are of good report; if there be any virtue, and if there be any praise, think on these things.
Philippians 4:8

El Elyon, in the Name of Your Son, Christ Jesus, I declare the Holy Spirit has unlimited access to my mind. By faith, I ask that He would govern my thoughts and cause them to be inclined to holy thoughts according to Philippians 4:8.

Thank You, God, for strengthening me so I do not grieve You with meditating on impure thoughts. I trust that thou wilt keep me in perfect peace as my mind is stayed on thee. Amen.

Day Fifty-Two

Prophetic Dreams

In a dream, in a vision of the night, when deep sleep falleth upon men, in slumberings upon the bed; Then He openeth the ears of men, and sealeth their instruction, that He may withdraw man from his purpose, and hide pride from man. Job 33:15-17

Dear Spirit of God, in Jesus' Name, today I pray to remind You of Scriptures which have encouraged and strengthen me. Particularly it is about dreams in the Word.

I praise You for using divine dreams to speak to Potiphar's wife, King Solomon, Joseph, and to Jesus' earthly father, Joseph. I praise You for faithfully continuing to speak prophetically in dreams to the Church.

I pray You would give me a heart to honor Your dreams as You reveal Your will for me and my family. May I ask that as You open my ears and seal Your instructions while I am asleep; You also protect the dream realm and preserve its holiness? Thank You for this honor to have You speak to me when I am asleep, Kind God. In Jesus' Name, I pray, Amen.

Day Fifty-Three

Return the hearts to You, O God

And he shall turn the heart of the fathers to the children, and the heart of the children to their fathers, lest I come and smite the earth with a curse. Malachi 4:6

God of Mercy, thank You for Your Son, the Risen Lord who have set me free.

Early in this morning, I come before You to cry out for Your mercy and plea with You to continue to heal and unite nations.

And Father, may You turn the hearts that have turned away from You back to You according to Malachi 4:6? In Jesus' Name, I pray, Amen.

Day Fifty-Four

Victory at Midnight

At midnight I will rise to give thanks unto thee because of thy righteous judgments. Psalm 119:62

Jehovah God, I give You praise, and honor for hearing this prayer according to 1 John 5:14-15. I praise You that the midnight hour which begins the third prayer watch is also an hour of favor for deliverance. Father, it is interesting that "Chetsiy," the Hebrew word for midnight is defined in the *Strong's Concordance* as midst, middle and midnight.

How great it is then that Your only Begotten Son, the Lion of Judah have established the midnight hour for a time that He enters in the midst of my praise to end the spiritual war oppressing me.

In this new day, I thank You for the Spirit of God's faithfulness to give me strength to awake at midnight to give You thanks and sing praises. Thank You for my deliverance and victory in Jesus Christ according to Acts 10:38. In Jesus' Name, Amen.

Day Fifty-Five

Securing my heavenly assignments

Thou shalt also decree a thing, and it shall be established unto thee: and the light shall shine upon thy ways. Job 22:28

Father of Glory, I ascribe to thee the glory due Your Name and worship You in the splendor of Your holiness. For a day in Your Courts is better than a thousand.

I thank You for the authority that You in Your goodness have given to me to reign with the King of Kings and Lord of Lords. And in His Name, I exercise dominion and authority over spiritual wickedness in high places.

I put You in remembrance of Your Word in the Book of Job, Chapter 22, verse 28: "Thou shalt also decree a thing, and it shall be established unto thee and the light shall shine upon thy ways."

Therefore, Jehovah Gibbor, I decree that the light shall shine upon my ways. I decree the spirit of Haman sent to dethrone me from my heavenly assignments is destroyed and hung on its own gallows. I decree the enemy' plan against me have been overruled by the King of Glory.

Thy Kingdom come, Thy will be done in earth, as it is in heaven. In the Name of Jesus Christ, I seal this prayer, Amen.

Day Fifty-Six

Honoring God's Holy Calendar

Now about the midst of the feast Jesus went up into the temple, and taught. John 7:14

Holy God, we give unto You all the praise, glory and honor. We declare that Ye are righteous in all Your ways and holy in all Your works. And we bless You for thy Word which remind us that You are nigh to all who call upon You in truth.

In John 7:37, the Scripture reads: "In the last day, that great day of the feast, Jesus stood and cried, saying, 'If any man thirst, let him come unto Me, and drink.'" We thank You for Your Word and declare we thirst after Your holiness and righteousness.

Certainly, God, we are grateful to our Master for teaching us in the Gospels to honor and observe the Feasts. We are grateful to read that these most Holy Days on Your Calendar You have commanded of us to observe in the Old Testament.

Wonder & Glory

Therefore, we ask You to come and be within our midst as we seek to honor You in our worship and giving during the holy season of Rosh Hashanah. Holy Spirit, we beseech You to give us grace to understand the deep things of God and the life of Christ when He walked on earth.

Let us have the honor to Feast with You, God. Together we will bless and reverence Your Holy Name. In Jesus' Name, Amen.

Day Fifty-Seven

Gratitude for Your meat in due season

These wait all upon thee; that thou mayest give them their meat in due season. Psalm 104:27

Holy Father, we arise to give You praise for it is because of Your mercies that we are not consumed and Your compassions fail us not.

In the dew of this morning of Your great faithfulness, we are grateful to enter into a most holy season on Your Calendar. We are honored to worship You again at this hour and sing of Your power and mercy, O Lord of Hosts.

We remain astonished at Your Word in Psalm 104:27, that Thou hast promised to give us meat in due season. Therefore, knowing of the open portals in this holy time; we shall wait upon You to fulfill this Word in this season.

Abba, thank You for inclining Your Ear to our prayers. In Christ Jesus, Name. Amen.

Day Fifty-Eight

Let us keepeth no account of wrongdoings

It does not act disgracefully, it does not seek its own benefit; it is not provoked, does not keep an account of a wrong suffered.
1 Corinthians 13:5

Holy God, who Hearest prayers in the multitude of Your mercies we ask that You incline thine Ear to our voice and supplications. Hear our cry as we put you in remembrance of Your promise that what things soever we desire, when we pray, believe that we receive them, and we shall have them. And when we stand praying, forgive, if we have ought against any that You may forgive us of our trespasses.

Father, we forgive those that have hurt, abandoned, rejected, dishonored, gossiped and slandered us. We ask You for more grace to keep no account of wrongs suffered according to First Corinthians 13:5.

Thank You, Loving God, for giving us Your Heart to forgive and love purely. We bless and reverence You. In Jesus Christ Name, Amen.

Day Fifty-Nine

Remember the lost, Father

No man can come to Me, except the Father which hath sent Me draw him: and I will raise him up at the last day. John 6:44

Eternal Father, I offer my sacrifices of praise to You who is holy, and who lead me in truth for thou art alone the God of my salvation. In this dawn of the morning, I am in awe of You as I meditate on Your glorious splendor and power which causes the mountains to melt like wax at Your presence.

I ask that You, The God of Might send an increase of the manifestations of Your signs and wonders in the earth. Would you remember how You performed Your signs wondrously at the Birth of Your only Begotten, Son, our Lord Jesus? May You in Your generosity manifest similar signs and wonders to the lost souls to draw them to Jesus according to John 6:44.

Thank You, Gracious Lord, for receiving my prayer and for the Lord Jesus, whom I love. Amen.

Day Sixty

Manifest the Latter Rain Glory

The glory of this latter house shall be greater than of the former, saith the LORD of hosts: and in this place will I give peace, saith the LORD of hosts. Haggai 2:9

Father of Glory, may You in Your generosity Hearest my prayer as I ask of thee for the latter rain glory according to Zechariah 10:1, and Haggai 2:9? Would You manifest Your wonder and glory for Your Children to see in this generation? How I desire for You to manifest Your glory, signs, and wonders in the earth. For the earth is Yours, God, and the fullness thereof.

I pray that You would grant me the grace to behold Your wonder and glory with a heart of humility, lowliness and meekness. Keep my heart from being lifted up in pride and cause my eyes to be fastened upon You whom I love with all of my heart, soul, mind and strength.

Thank You, God, for the eyewitnesses who will also behold of Your wonder, signs and Majesty. In Christ Jesus' Name, Amen.

Now unto Him that is able to keep you from falling, and to present you faultless before the presence of His glory with exceeding joy. To the only wise God our Savior, be glory and majesty, dominion and power, both now and ever. Amen.

Contact Apostle Tonya

Website: www.apostletonya.org
Blog: www.apostletonya.video.blog
Instagram: @apostledrtonya
YouTube: @apostletonya

Made in the USA
Columbia, SC
12 February 2024